ENVIRONMENTAL ACTS

DR. B. KARPAGAM, DR. P. ADWIN JOSE DR. J. RAJESH, DR. M. SANKARGANESH AND DR. G. RAJAGOPAL

Copyright © Dr. B. Karpagam, Dr. P. Adwin Jose Dr. J. Rajesh, Dr. M. Sankarganesh and Dr. G. Rajagopal
All Rights Reserved.

This book has been self-published with all reasonable efforts taken to make the material error-free by the author. No part of this book shall be used, reproduced in any manner whatsoever without written permission from the author, except in the case of brief quotations embodied in critical articles and reviews.

The Author of this book is solely responsible and liable for its content including but not limited to the views, representations, descriptions, statements, information, opinions and references ["Content"]. The Content of this book shall not constitute or be construed or deemed to reflect the opinion or expression of the Publisher or Editor. Neither the Publisher nor Editor endorse or approve the Content of this book or guarantee the reliability, accuracy or completeness of the Content published herein and do not make any representations or warranties of any kind, express or implied, including but not limited to the implied warranties of merchantability, fitness for a particular purpose. The Publisher and Editor shall not be liable whatsoever for any errors, omissions, whether such errors or omissions result from negligence, accident, or any other cause or claims for loss or damages of any kind, including without limitation, indirect or consequential loss or damage arising out of use, inability to use, or about the reliability, accuracy or sufficiency of the information contained in this book.

Made with ♥ on the Notion Press Platform
www.notionpress.com

Contents

Foreword

Environmental laws play a crucial role in shaping our interactions with the natural world, ensuring the sustainability of our planet for future generations. The development and enforcement of these laws are integral to addressing the myriad challenges posed by pollution, climate change, biodiversity loss, and resource depletion. As our understanding of environmental science evolves, so too must our legal frameworks, adapting to new realities and scientific advancements.

This book, "Environmental Laws," seeks to provide a comprehensive overview of the legal principles, policies, and regulations that govern our relationship with the environment. It aims to equip readers with a deep understanding of the historical evolution, current state, and future trajectory of environmental legislation. By exploring key statutes, case laws, and international treaties, this book offers a detailed examination of the mechanisms in place to protect our air, water, soil, and ecosystems.

Written with an academic audience in mind, "Environmental Laws" is designed to serve as a valuable resource for students, educators, legal practitioners, policymakers, and anyone with a vested interest in environmental protection. Each chapter delves into specific areas of environmental law, supported by real-world examples, critical analyses, and discussion questions to facilitate deeper engagement and reflection.

As we stand at a critical juncture in the fight against environmental degradation, it is my hope that this book will inspire and empower readers to contribute to the ongoing efforts to create a more sustainable and just world. The journey towards robust and effective environmental laws is a collective endeavor, requiring informed and dedicated individuals. Let this book be a stepping stone on that path.

Preface

The genesis of this book, "Environmental Laws," lies in the growing recognition of the pivotal role that legal frameworks play in the stewardship of our natural environment. Over the past few decades, the escalating impacts of industrialization, urbanization, and global climate change have underscored the necessity for robust and dynamic legal instruments that can address environmental challenges on both national and international levels.

This book is a culmination of extensive research and analysis, aimed at providing a comprehensive exploration of environmental laws. It is intended to serve as a foundational text for students of environmental science, law, and policy, as well as a reference guide for practitioners and policymakers engaged in environmental protection and sustainable development.

"Environmental Laws" is structured to offer a detailed examination of the major statutes, regulations, and international agreements that govern environmental protection. Each chapter delves into specific aspects of environmental law, including air and water quality, waste management, biodiversity conservation, and climate change mitigation. By integrating case studies, legislative histories, and critical commentaries, this book seeks to elucidate the complexities and nuances of environmental legislation.

In writing this book, I have endeavored to highlight the interconnectedness of environmental issues and the importance of a holistic approach to legal regulation. The aim is to foster a deeper understanding of how laws can be leveraged to achieve environmental justice and sustainability. I hope that this book will inspire readers to critically engage with the subject matter and contribute to the ongoing discourse on environmental law and policy.

I extend my gratitude to the numerous scholars, practitioners, and students whose insights and feedback have enriched this work. It is my sincere hope that "Environmental Laws" will serve as a valuable resource for all those committed to safeguarding our planet for future generations.

Prologue

In the heart of our modern era, we stand at a crossroads where the decisions we make today will echo through the centuries to come. The unprecedented scale of environmental challenges—ranging from climate change to biodiversity loss, from air and water pollution to unsustainable resource consumption—demands a robust and cohesive legal response. It is within this context that "Environmental Laws" finds its relevance and urgency.

This book emerges from a deep-seated commitment to understanding and addressing the intricate legal frameworks that govern our relationship with the environment. The journey to compile this work has been both enlightening and sobering, revealing the profound impact that well-crafted laws can have on the preservation and restoration of our natural world. Yet, it also highlights the gaps and shortcomings that persist in our legal systems, calling for continual evolution and enforcement.

"Environmental Laws" is more than a mere compilation of statutes and regulations; it is a narrative that traces the evolution of environmental legal thought, from its nascent stages to its current complexities. It explores the interplay between environmental science and policy, the role of international cooperation, and the vital importance of public participation in environmental governance.

As you delve into the chapters ahead, you will encounter a blend of historical insights, contemporary analyses, and forward-looking perspectives. Each section is crafted to provide not only an understanding of the legal mechanisms in place but also a critical appraisal of their effectiveness and areas for improvement. It is my hope that this prologue sets the stage for a deeper engagement with the material, fostering a sense of responsibility and empowerment in the quest for environmental justice.

In presenting this book, I am reminded of the words of Rachel Carson, whose seminal work "Silent Spring" awakened the world to the perils of environmental neglect: “The human race is challenged more than ever before to demonstrate our mastery, not over nature but of ourselves.” May this book serve as a testament to that challenge, and as a guide for all who seek to meet it.

CHAPTER I

INTRODUCTION

Environment plays a vital role in human life as well as in the development of society. With growing technological advancement and industrialization, the purity of the environment has been threatened to an appalling extent. The need to protect and improve the environment is so compelling for the peaceful survival of mankind and other life forms on planet Earth that right to environment has emerged as a human right. Over the last two decades, the Indian judiciary has fostered an extensive and innovative approach to environmental rights in the country. Complex matters of environmental management have been resolved and consequently a series of innovative procedural remedies have evolved to accompany this new substantive right. The new environmental right is therefore championed as a legal gateway to speedy and inexpensive legal remedy. With the rapid increase in industrialization and human needs, environment has been badly suffered. The importance of protection as well as conservation of environment alongwith sustainable use of natural resources is reflected really well in the constitutional framework of India. The Environmental laws in India give huge importance to maintain an ecological balance of environment by safeguarding the forests and wildlife of the country.

The national expansion of right to life was recognized even in the absence of a specific reference to direct violations of the fundamental right. Placed in a nutshell, the human right culture has percolated down to Indian human right regime within a short period of time. An interdisciplinary approach to environmental protection may be another reason for the operation of the right to healthy environment. This has been undertaken through international environmental treaties & conventions, national legislative measures and in judicial responses. The necessity for environmental protection and conservation, as well as the sustainable use of natural resources, is reflected in India's constitutional framework and international commitments.

The environment is defined as the whole physical and biological system surrounding man and other organisms along with various factors influencing them. The factors are soil, air, water, light, temperature etc. These are called Abiotic factors. The Environment is our basic life support system and is composed of living beings, physical surroundings, and climatic conditions. Biotic refers to the world of living organisms, whereas Abiotic refers to the world of non-living elements. The Environment provides us the basic elements – air, water, food, and land which are essential for life to flourish on the Earth.

Our Environment comprises of three components – natural components (air, water, land & living things), human components (individual, family, community), and human-made components (roads, monuments, industries), and is a combination of natural and human-made phenomena. The Natural Environment could be further classified into four different domains- lithosphere, Hydrosphere, Biosphere, and Atmosphere.

SCOPE OF ENVIRONMENTAL STUDIES

Environmental studies discipline has multiple and multilevel scopes. This study is important and necessary not only for children but also for everyone. The scopes are summarized as follows:

- The study creates awareness among the people to know about various renewable and

  nonrenewable resources of the region.

- The endowment or potential, patterns of utilization and the balance of various resources available for future use in the state of a country are analyzed in the study.
- It provides the knowledge about ecological systems and cause and effect relationships.
- It provides necessary information about biodiversity richness and the potential dangers to the species of plants, animals and microorganisms in the environment.
- The study enables one to understand the causes and consequences due to natural and main induced disasters (flood, earthquake, landslide, cyclones etc.,) and pollutions and measures to minimize the effects.
- It enables one to evaluate alternative responses to environmental issues before deciding an alternative course of action.
- The study enables environmentally literate citizens (by knowing the environmental acts, rights, rules, legislations, etc.) to make appropriate

judgments and decisions for the protection and improvement of the earth.

- The study exposes the problems of over population, health, hygiene, etc. and the role of arts, science and technology in eliminating/ minimizing the evils from the society.
- The study tries to identify and develop appropriate and indigenous eco-friendly skills and

technologies to various environmental issues.

- It teaches the citizens the need for sustainable utilization of resources as these resources are inherited from our ancestors to the younger generating without deteriorating their quality.
- The study enables theoretical knowledge into practice and the multiple uses of environment.

IMPORTANCE OF ENVIRONMENTAL STUDY

Environmental study is based upon a comprehensive view of various environmental systems. It aims to make the citizens competent to do scientific work and to find out practical solutions to current environmental problems. The citizens acquire the ability to analyze the environmental parameters like the aquatic, terrestrial and atmospheric systems and their interactions with the biosphere.

- World population is increasing at an alarming rate especially in developing countries.
- The natural resources endowment in the earth is limited.
- The methods and techniques of exploiting natural resources are advanced.
- The resources are over-exploited and there is no foresight of leaving the resources to the future generations.
- The unplanned exploitation of natural resources lead to pollution of all types and at all levels.
- The pollution and degraded environment seriously affect the health of all living things on earth, including man.
- The people should take a combined responsibility for the deteriorating environment and begin to take appropriate actions to space the earth.

- Education and training are needed to save the biodiversity and species extinction.
- The urban area, coupled with industries, is major sources of pollution.
- The number and area extinct under protected area should be increased so that the wild life is protected at least in these sites.
- The study enables the people to understand the complexities of the environment and need for the people to adapt appropriate activities and pursue sustainable development, which are harmonious with the environment.
- The study motivates students to get involved in community action, and to participate in

  various environmental and management projects.

- It is a high time to reorient educational systems and curricula towards these needs.
- Environmental studies take a multidisciplinary approach to the study of human interactions with the natural environment. It integrates different approaches of the humanities, social sciences, biological sciences and physical sciences and applies these approaches to investigate environmental concerns.
- Environmental study is a key instrument for bringing about the changes in the knowledge, values, behaviors and lifestyles required to achieve sustainability and stability within and among countries.

PUBLIC AWARENESS IN PROTECTING THE ENVIRONMENT

- Since our environment is getting degraded due to human activities, we need to do something about it to sustain the quality.
- We often feel that government should take proper measuring steps.
- But all of us are equally responsible to protect our environment. Hence public awareness needs to be created.
- Both print media and electronic media can strongly influence public opinion. Politicians should respond positively to a strong publicly supported activity.
- NGOs can take active role in creating awareness from grass root levels to the top-most policy decision makers.
- Environment is an integration of both living and non-living organisms.

- Water, air, soil, minerals, wild life, grass lands, forests, oceans, agriculture are all life supporting systems.
- Since these natural resources are limited, and human activities are the causative factors for environmental degradation, each one of us need to feel responsible to protect the environment.
- Increasing population, Urbanization and poverty have generated pressure on the natural resources and lead to a degradation of the environment.
- To prevent the environment from further degradation, the Supreme Court has ordered and initiated environmental protection awareness through government and non-government agencies to take part in protecting our environment.
- Environmental pollution cannot be prevented by laws alone. Public participation is equally important with regard to environmental protection.
- Environmental Education is a process of learning by giving an overall perspective of knowledge and awareness of the environment.
- It sensitizes the society about environmental issues and challenges interested individuals to develop skills and expertise thereby providing appropriate solutions.
- Climate change, loss of biodiversity, declining fisheries, ozone layer depletion, illegal trade of endangered species, destruction of habitats, land degradation, depleting ground water supplies, introduction of alien species, environmental pollution, solid waste disposal, storm water and sewage disposal pose a serious threat to ecosystems in forest, rural, urban and marine ecosystems.
- Both formal and informal education on the environment will give the interested individual the knowledge, values, skills and tools needed to face the environmental challenges on a local and global level.

Ecosystem is the basic functional unit of ecology. Ecology is the study of relationships between organisms and their environment.

ENVIRONMENTAL ETHICS

Over exploitation of forests, land, water as well as various living components of biosphere and failure to tackle the problem of pollution and environmental degradation are exposing the humanly to the thread of a global environment crisis. Therefore, human beings are ethically responsible for the preservation of the world's ecological integrity. The environment ethics literally means conscious efforts to protect environment and to maintain its stability from the pollutants. Following are some of the ways to safeguard environment.

ETHICAL GUIDELINES

- Love & honor the earth.
- Should be grateful to plants & animals.
- Should not waste your resources.
- Should not steal from future generation.
- Should not pollute & hold other living things.
- Should not consume more materials.
- Should share the precious earth resources.

CHAPTER II

ECOSYSTEM

An ecosystem is a dynamic network of living organisms (plants, animals, and microorganisms) and their physical environment (soil, water, and air), interacting as a cohesive unit. These interactions facilitate energy flow and nutrient cycling, essential for maintaining balance and functionality. Ecosystems can be terrestrial (forests, grasslands) or aquatic (lakes, oceans), each supporting diverse life forms. Biodiversity within ecosystems ensures resilience against disturbances and provides vital services like pollination and water purification. However, human activities such as deforestation and pollution threaten these systems, making conservation efforts crucial for sustaining life on Earth.

STRUCTURE AND FUNCTIONS OF AN ECOSYSTEM

The term structure refers to various components, which combine to produce an ecosystem. An ecosystem has biotic and abiotic components.

BIOTIC COMPONENT

They are living components present in the ecosystem. The plants, animals and microorganisms present in an ecosystem form the biotic component. It includes producers, consumers and decomposers.

ABIOTIC COMPONENT

They are non-living components present in the ecosystem.

1. Physical components Example: soil type, temperature, rain wind etc.
2. Chemical components Example: nutrients like H, O, S, C, P present in water and soil.

The physical and chemical components of an ecosystem constitute the abiotic structure.

The biotic and abiotic components are linked through energy flow in the ecosystem.

FUNCTION OF AN ECOSYSTEM

Every ecosystem performs in a systematic manner. It receives energy from the sun and passes it on to various biotic components and life depends on these factors. The important functions of an ecosystem are,

- It decides the food chain, food web and the tropical structure.
- It helps in energy flow.
- Cycling of nutrients like N, P, S occurs in the ecosystem.
- It helps in primary and secondary production.
- It plays a major role in regulation and development of biosphere.

PRODUCERS, CONSUMERS AND DECOMPOSERS

These are the biotic components of an ecosystem.

a. Producers: These are mainly green plants which synthesize food by photosynthesis using CO_2 present in air, in the presence of sunlight and chlorophyll. Producers are also called **autotrophs.**

b. Consumers: The organisms which depend on other organisms for food are called consumers. Example. Goat, Cow

Primary consumers – They depend directly on producers for food. Example: Cow, goat, sheep.

Secondary consumers – They feed on the primary consumers Example: Lion, Tiger.

Tertiary consumers – They feed on both plants and animals for food Example: Fox, Man.

Saprotropes – They depend on dead organic matter for food.

c. Decomposers: They derive their nutrients by breaking down the complex organic molecules to simple organic compounds.

Example: Bacteria, Fungi

Photosynthesis

The CO_2 is taken up by the open pores on the surface of leaf known as stomata guarded by the guard cells.

The plant body also takes up many other things such as water and sunlight for preparation of its food. This could be expressed as follows-

ENERGY FLOW IN AN ECOSYSTEM

The process involving transfer of energy from one tropic level to another tropic level is known as Energy flow. The energy flow is always **uni-directional**. That is, energy flows from producer to consumer and then to decomposer and not in the reverse direction. Sun is the source of energy for most organisms to carry out processes required to sustain life. Considerable amount of energy is lost during energy flow from one level to another level.

Out of the total energy captured by green plants [producers], only a minimum amount is transferred to the next tropic level, the remaining is dissipated in the form of radiant heat. Only 10 % of energy produced by producers are utilized by consumers [herbivores] occupying the second tropic level. Most energy is lost via respiration by herbivores. In 1942, Lindemann proposed the energy flow model in an ecosystem [single channel flow].

At carnivore level, about 60 % of energy intake is consumed in metabolic activities and the remaining becomes part of the unutilized sediments. Thus, energy flow is unidirectional and obeys the **FIRST AND SECOND LAWS OF THERMODYNAMICS**. The First Law of Thermodynamics states that energy cannot be created or destroyed; it can only be converted from one form to another. The second law of thermodynamics states that when energy is converted from one form to another, some energy is lost and efficiency decreases. There is a progressive reduction in energy with increasing tropic level [second law of Thermodynamics] due to dissipation of heat in metabolic activities and respiration.

ECOLOGICAL SUCCESSION

The progressive replacement of one community by another till the development of stable community in a particular area is called ecological succession.

- Ecological succession starting in water resource like pond, is a *Hydrarch*.
- Succession starts in an area of adequate moisture is a *Mesarch*
- Succession starting in a dry area is a *Xerarch*.

Various processes involved in ecological succession

The **process of succession** takes place in a systematic order as follows;

- **Nudation** – Bare area without any life forms.
- **Invasion** – Establishment of one or more species by dispersal of seeds which germinate and grow on land.
- **Competition** – As the number of individuals grow, there is inter-specific [different] and

  intra- specific [same] competition known as co action.

- **Reaction** – The living organisms grow, use water, nutrients and get modified to a large

  extent.

- **Stabilization** – The succession ultimately ends up with a more or less stable community

called Climax which is in equilibrium with environment.

FOOD CHAIN

The food chain is an ideal representation of flow of energy in the ecosystem.

In food chain, the plants or producers are consumed by only the primary consumers, primary consumers are fed by only the secondary consumers and so on. The producers that are capable to produce their own food are called autotrophs. Any food chain consists of three main tropic levels, viz., producers, consumers and decomposers.

Grass → Grasshopper → Frog → Hawk.

Grass → Grasshopper → Rat → Fox.

FOOD WEB

A food web is a graphical depiction of feeding connections among species of an ecological community. Food web includes food chains of a particular ecosystem. The food web is an illustration of various techniques of feeding that links the ecosystem.

The food web also explains the energy flow through species of a community as a result of their feeding relationships. All the food chains are interconnected and overlapping within an ecosystem and they constitute a food web. In natural environment or an ecosystem, the relationships between the food chains are interrelated. The web like structure if formed with the interlinked food chain and such matrix that is interconnected is known as a food web.

ECOLOGICAL PYRAMIDS

An ecological pyramid is a graphical representation outlined to show the biomass or bio productivity at each trophic level in a given ecosystem. These are trophic pyramid, energy pyramid, or sometimes food pyramid. Biomass is the quantity of living or organic matter present in an organism. Biomass pyramids represent the amount of biomass, and how much of it is present in the organisms at each trophic level.

Flow of energy through the food chain will be in a predictable way, entering at the base of the food chain, by photosynthesis in primary producers, and then moving up the food chain to higher trophic levels. However, the relationship between energy, biomass, and number can be complex by the growth form and size of organisms and ecological relationships occurring among trophic levels.

CHAPTER III

BIODIVERSITY

BIODIVERSITY

Biodiversity is the variety among living organisms from all sources including terrestrial, marine and other aquatic ecosystems.

CLASSIFICATION OR LEVELS OF BIODIVERSITY

The concept of biodiversity may be analyzed in 3 different levels. They are

1 Ecosystem diversity

2 Species diversity

3 Genetic diversity

Ecosystem or ecological diversity means the richness and complexity of a biological community, including tropic levels, ecological processes, food webs and material recycling. The ecosystems also show variations with respect to physical parameters like moisture, temperature, altitude etc. Example: River ecosystem

Species diversity The variation found within the population of a species or between different species of a community is species diversity. Example: Plant species: Apple, Mango

Animal species: Lion, Tiger

Genetic diversity Genes are the units of hereditary information transmitted from one generation to another. When genes within the same species show new combinations, it is called genetic variability. Eg: Rice varieties, teak wood varieties.

INDIA AS MEGA-DIVERSE BIODIVERSITY

Biodiversity has three aspects, viz. genetics, species and ecosystem. India is recognized to be uniquely rich in all these three aspects. The country has a rich heritage of biodiversity, encompassing a wide spectrum of habitats from tropical rainforests to alpine vegetation, and from temperate forests to coastal wetlands. Almost all the bio geographical regions of the world are represented here in India. With a mere 2.4% of the total land area of the world, the known biodiversity of India contributes 8.22% of the known global biodiversity. India is one of the twelve mega-diversity nations of the world accounting for 7.31% of the global faunal and 10.88% of the global floral total species. Currently available data place

India in the tenth position in the world and fourth in the Asia in plant diversity. In terms of number of mammalian species, the country ranks tenth in the world; and in terms of endemic species of higher vertebrates, it ranks eleventh. In terms of number of species contributed to agriculture and animal husbandry, it ranks seventh in the world.

THE REASONS FOR GREATER BIODIVERSITY IN THE TROPICS

The centers of greatest biodiversity tend to be in the tropics.

- Tropical areas receive more solar energy over the year. Therefore, tropical communities are more productive resulting in a greater resource base that can support a wider range of species.
- Warm temperatures and high humidity of tropical areas provide favourable environmental conditions for many species that are unable to survive in the temperate areas.
- Over geological times, the tropics have had a more stable climate than the temperate areas. In tropics, therefore, local species continued to thrive and live there itself; whereas, in temperate zones, they tend to disperse to other areas.
- There has been more time for tropical communities to evolve as they are older than temperate ones. This could have allowed tropical communities greater degree of specialization and local adaptation to occur.
- In tropics, the greater pressure from pests, parasites and diseases does not allow any single species to dominate. Thus, there is opportunity for many species to coexist. In temperate areas, on the other hand, there is reduced pressure from pests, parasites and diseases due to cold, and there is one or a few dominating species that exclude many other species.
- In tropics, higher rates of out crossing among plants may lead to higher levels of genetic variability.

VALUES OF BIODIVERSITY

- The value of a particular species will be known only when it is not available. Each organism plays a crucial role in the ecological balance of the ecosystem. A rich biodiversity is the wealth of a nation. We get the following benefits from rich biodiversity. The components of biodiversity are the source of all our food and many of our medicines, fibers, fuels, and industrial products. The direct uses of the components of biodiversity contribute substantially to the economy.

1. **Consumptive value**

Food

A large number of wild plants are consumed by human beings as food [80,000 edible plant species]. About 4000 native plant and animal species are used in preparing food, medicine and other valuable products.

Drugs and Medicine

About 75 % of the World's population depends upon plants or plant extracts for medicine. The wonder drug, Penicillin used as an antibiotic is derived from Penicillium. Quinine, the cure for malaria is obtained from the bark of Cinchona tree. A large number of marine animals are supposed to possess anti – cancer properties.

Wild species of plants and animals have long been the source of important pharmaceutical products. Natural products play a central role in traditional healthcare systems.

Fuel

Our forests have been used since ages for fuel wood. The fossil fuels like Coal, Petroleum and natural gas are also used.

2. **Productive value**

These refer to the commercial value of products that are marketed and sold, such as meat, timber, fish, ivory, medicinal plants etc. Many industries are dependent on productive use of biodiversity. Example: Paper and pulp industries, plywood industry, silk industry, leather industry, pearl industry etc. Developing countries in Asia, Africa and Latin America are the richest biodiversity centers where wild life products are smuggled and marketed in large quantities to Western countries and China, Hong Kong where export of cat skins and snake skins is a booming business.

3. **Social Value**

These are values associated with the social life, customs, religion and spiritual aspects of the people. Many plants like tulsi, Lotus etc., are considered holy and sacred in our country. The leaves, fruits or flowers of these plants are used in worship. The life of the tribal people in forests, their songs, dance and customs are closely related with wild life. Thus biodiversity has distinct social value attached with different societies.

4. **Ethical Value**

This involves issues like respecting the nature beyond the supremacy of humans. It is based on high moral principles and compassion towards all living forms. India's rich biodiversity could be due to this ethical view from the Vedic period. As we know, plants and animals are praised with Gods and given due credentials. This means there is an ethical value or existence value attached to each species. Example:Kangaroo, Zebra, Giraffe

5. **Aesthetic Value**

Great aesthetic value (Eco-tourism) is attached to biodiversity. Millions of people enjoy hunting, fishing, camping wild-life watching and other natural activities. These activities provide stress-relief, good exercise and restores emotions. In many religions, nature is considered as God's creation and is being worshipped. Eco tourism is an aesthetic value of biodiversity and is estimated to generate good revenue annually.

6. **Optional Value**

This value includes potentials of biodiversity that are presently unknown and need to be explored. It is the value of knowing the existing resources in the biosphere which may one day prove to be an effective option in the future. Thus, the optional value of biodiversity suggests that any species may prove effective someday.

ENDANGERED AND ENDEMIC SPECIES

The areas which exhibit high species richness and species endemism are termed as hotspots of biodiversity. Most of the world's biodiversity concentrations are near the Equator, especially tropical rain forests. About 40 % of terrestrial plants and 25 % of vertebrate species are endemic and found in these hotspots. After tropical rain forests, the second highest number of endemic plant species is found in the Mediterranean. These **hotspots include the Western Amazon, Madagascar, North-eastern Australia, West Africa and Brazilian forests.** These are areas of high diversity, endemism and also threatened by human activities.

The areas therefore isolated by water, desert or mountains have high concentrations of unique species and biodiversity. There are 18 hotspots identified worldwide. The Indian hotspots are not only rich in floral wealth and endemic species of plants but also reptiles, amphibians, butterflies and some mammals. The following hotspots are identified in India;

1. ***Eastern Himalayas***

They display varied topography and have numerous deep isolated valleys in Sikkim rich in endemic plant species. The forests cover one-third of area in Eastern Himalayas. Out of the world's recorded flora, 30 % are endemic to India of which 35000 are in the Himalayas.

2. ***Western Ghats***

It extends along 17000km strip of forests in Maharashtra, Karnataka, Tamilnadu and Kerala. It has 40 % of total endemic plant species. And also 62 % amphibians and 50 % lizards are endemic to Western Ghats. The major centers of diversity are Agastyamalai hills and Silent Valley. Only 6.8 % of original forests exist today and we have lost a huge proportion of biodiversity.

- The list of endangered species of plants and animals are published in the **Red Data Book** by the IUCN [International Union for Conservation of Nature and Natural resources]. The red data symbolizes the warning signal for the species endangered and become extinct in the near future. In India, nearly 450 plant species have been identified as endangered species. Existence of about 150 mammals and 150 species of birds is estimated to be threatened.
- Extinct – If a species is not seen in the wild for the past 50 years at a stretch it is said to be extinct. Example: Passenger pigeon
- Endangered – When the number of species is drastically reduced to a critical level and is in the immediate danger of extinction it is said to be endangered. Example: Snow leopard.
- Vulnerable – If the population of a species is facing continuous decline due to habitat destruction or over exploitation, it is said to be vulnerable.
- Rare species– The species which is localized within restricted areas and thinly scattered is a rare species.
- Some of the animals grouped under threatened species are; a. *Reptiles* – Green sea turtle, Tortoise, Python, Salt water crocodile etc. b. *Birds* – Wood Pigeon, White winged wood duck, etc. c. *Carnivorous mammals* – Indian wolf, Red fox, Red panda, snow leopard, Tiger, Goldencat, desert cat etc. d. *Primates* – Capped monkey etc. e. *Plants* – Species of orchids, medicinal plant like serpentine, sandalwood tree
- The Botanical survey of India has estimated that about 10 % of higher plants are threatened. India possesses a large number of endemic species. Out of 47,000 plant species 7000 are endemic. Some of the important endemic flora include Sapria himalayana, Uvaria lurida etc. A large number of species of animals in our country is endemic. About 62 % amphibians and 50 % lizards are endemic to Western Ghats. Different species of monitor lizards reticulated Python and Indian Salamander are

some endemic species of our country.

CONSERVATION OF BIODIVERSITY

Biodiversity conservation is the protection and management of biodiversity to obtain resources for sustainable development. It is defined as "Protection, restoration, and management of biodiversity in order to derive sustainable benefits for present and future generations.". Or, it can also be defined as, "the totality of genes, species, and ecosystems in a defined area.".

Biodiversity conservation has three main objectives:

1.To preserve the diversity of species.

2.Sustainable utilization of species and ecosystem.

3.To maintain life-supporting systems and essential ecological processes.

Biodiversity refers to the variability of life on earth. It can be conserved in the following ways:

In-situ Conservation

Ex-situ Conservation

I. In – situ Conservation (with in habitat)

This is achieved by protection of wild flora and fauna in nature itself. Example: Biosphere reserves, National Parks, Sanctuaries, Reserve forests etc. This helps in conserving vast number of species of living organisms and provides opportunities to evolve.

1. **Biosphere reserves**: They conserve some representation ecosystems on the whole for a long term. It has been set for ecological research and habitat preservation. Biosphere reserve consist of large number of genetic diversity. These are national governments nominated sites, large areas (often up to 5000 square km) of an ecosystem where the traditional lifestyle and natural habitat of the inhabitants of that ecosystem are protected. They are mostly open to tourists and researchers.

2. ***National Park***: It is an area dedicated for conservation of wild life along with the environment. These are limited reserves maintained by the government for the conservation of wildlife as well as the environment. Human activities are prohibited in national parks and they are solely dedicated to the protection of natural fauna of the area. They mostly occupy an area of 100-500 square km. The national parks may even be within a biosphere reserve. These are small reserves that are protected and maintained by the government. Its boundaries are well protected, where human activities such as grazing, forestry, habitat, and cultivation are restricted. Usually they are tourist centers and aim at conservation of

particular species of wild life. Some of the national parks of our country are

3. Wild life Sanctuaries: Wildlife Sanctuaries are protected areas meant only for the conservation of wild animals. A few human activities such as cultivation, wood collection, and other forest product collection are allowed here, but they must not interfere with the conservation of the animals. Tourist visits are also allowed in these areas. There are a total of 551 wildlife sanctuaries in India. These are the places where only wild animals can be found. Certain human activities like timber harvesting, cultivation, collection of woods, and other forest products are permitted unless they interfere with the conservation project. Recreation tourism is also permitted. Example:

4.Gene Sanctuary

Gene sanctuary is a conservation area reserved only for plants. India has its only gene sanctuary set up in Garo Hills of Meghalaya for the conservation of wild species of Citrus. Plans to open more such sanctuaries are underway. For plants, there is a gene sanctuary for citrus [lemon family] and for pitcher plant [insect eating plant] in North east India. For protection and conservation of certain animals, there have been specific projects in our country.

The in-situ conservation has several advantages. Following are the important advantages of in-situ conservation:

- It is a cost-effective and convenient method of conserving biodiversity.
- A large number of living organisms can be conserved simultaneously.
- Since the organisms are in a natural ecosystem, they can evolve better and can easily adjust to different environmental conditions.

II. Ex-situ Conservation (Outside the habitat)

This is done by establishment of gene banks, seed banks, zoos, botanical gardens etc. This type of conservation is done for crop varieties; wild crops etc. for future crop improvement or afforestation programmes. In India, the following gene bank / seed facilities are adopted;

Ex-situ conservation of biodiversity involves the breeding and maintenance of endangered species in artificial ecosystems such as zoos, nurseries, botanical gardens, gene banks, etc. There is less competition for food, water and space among the organisms.

NBPGR [National Bureau of Plant Genetic Resources] – Located at New Delhi. Varieties of rice, tomato, onion, carrot, chilly, tobacco, poppy etc. havebeenpreservedsuccessfullyinliquidnitrogen for several years.

NBAGR [National Bureau of Animal Genetic Resources] – LocatedatKarnal, Haryana. Itpreservessemenofdomesticatedanimals.

NFPTCR [National Facilityfor Plant Tissue culture Repository] – For conserving varieties of crop plants by tissue culture.

Ex-situ conservation has the following advantages:

- The animals are provided with a longer time and breeding activity.
- The species bred in captivity can be reintroduced in the wild.
- Genetic techniques can be used for the preservation of endangered species.

Need for Biodiversity Conservation

- Various types of conservation methods ensure a healthy ecosystem.
- A healthy ecosystem means a clean and healthy environment, smooth running food chains, availability of resources, and so on.
- Human beings are also majorly dependent on the environment for basic necessities and wellbeing.
- We are interdependent on a variety of species of plants and animals for a living. Hence it is very important to conserve these species and their ecosystems which are threatened by many human activities.
- A threat to biodiversity poses a threat to humankind.
- It can be the cause of various grave problems like pollution, habitat loss, resource exploitation, climate change, species extinction, disease outbreak, and so on.
- For economic and various life support reasons, it is very important to protect and preserve biodiversity.

Strategies for Biodiversity Conservation

Following are the important strategies for biodiversity conservation:

- All the varieties of food, timber plants, livestock, microbes and agricultural animals should be conserved.
- All the economically important organisms should be identified and conserved.
- Unique ecosystems should be preserved first.
- The resources should be utilized efficiently.

- Poaching and hunting of wild animals should be prevented.
- The reserves and protected areas should be developed carefully.
- The levels of pollutants should be reduced in the environment.
- Deforestation should be strictly prohibited.
- Environmental laws should be followed strictly.
- The useful and endangered species of plants and animals should be conserved in their nature as well as artificial habitats.
- Public awareness should be created regarding biodiversity conservation and its importance.

CHAPTER IV

ENVIRONMENTAL ACTS

The need for the existence of environmental laws and their strict implementation is paramount for conservation and protection of the environment including the wildlife. Part IV of the Indian Constitution (Article 48-A, Directive Principles of State Policy) explicitly states that the government must work to maintain and improve the environment as well as the country's wildlife. Furthermore, the Constitution under Part IV-A (Article 51-A, Fundamental Duties) casts a duty upon the citizens of India to preserve and improve the natural environment of the land. In addition to this, India has made several international commitments and signed treaties with regard to protection of the environment which it must uphold and honor.

One of the most important bodies of the Government of India that deals environmental protection is the Ministry of Environment and Forests (MoEF) which came into force in 1985 after the prominent Stockholm Conference, 1972. MoEF is concerned with regulating and preserving the natural environment and legislating on the legal and regulatory framework for the same. The Ministry of Environment and Forests along with the Pollution Control Board form the administrative crux of this sector. Even though India has made significant progress in improving the environmental conditions, there are still some obstacles that it is yet to overcome.

The environmental sector has advanced and secured a vital position in the global as well as Indian contexts, many more improvements and reforms are yet to be made to receive positive environmental outputs in a larger sense rather than being led by the approach that environmental progression may hurt the socio-economic system. Apart from international laws, every country has enacted laws regarding environment protection, pollution control etc. In India, there are several acts for environment protection that says protection of environment is the duty of government. The importance of environmental legislation is in that without adequate regulations and laws, environment conservation cannot be realized [3] environment. Creating environmental awareness and promoting environmental education are the means to ensure that humans do not degrade environment but conserve it for the future.

MAJOR ENVIRONMENT POLICIES AND LEGISLATIONS IN INDIA

The Ministry of Environment and Forests is the nodal body in the Central Government's administrative structure for planning, promotion, coordination, and oversight of environmental and forestry programmes. The Ministry is also the Nodal agency in the country for the United Nations Environment Programme (UNEP). The principal activities undertaken by Ministry of Environment & Forests, consist of conservation & survey of flora, fauna, forests and Wildlife, prevention & control of pollution, afforestation & regeneration of degraded areas and protection of environment, in the frame work of legislations. The main tools utilized for this include surveys, impact assessment, control of pollution, regeneration programmes, support to organizations, research to solve solutions and training to augment the requisite manpower, collection and dissemination of environmental information and creation of environmental awareness among all sectors of the country's population.

The Water (Prevention and Control of Pollution) Act of 1974 established the Central Pollution Control Board (CPCB), a governmental agency, in September 1974. The Air (Prevention and Control of Pollution) Act of 1981 also gave the CPCB powers and responsibilities. It serves as a field formation and also provides technical services to the Ministry of Environment and Forests of the provisions of the Environment (Protection) Act, 1986. The Water (Prevention and Control of Pollution) Act of 1974 and the Air (Prevention and Control of Pollution) Act of 1981 spell out the CPCB's main responsibilities, (i) to promote cleanliness of streams and wells in different areas of the States by prevention, control and abatement of water pollution, and (ii) to improve the country's air quality and to avoid, control, or reduce air pollution.

INDIA'S AGENCIES FOR MAKING ENVIRONMENTAL LAWS AND ENFORCEMENT

The Department of Science and Technology established a National Council of Environment Planning and Coordination in 1972. Additional group was made in 1980 to explore present ecological regulation and organizational kit and to create endorsements on how to support standing commandments and conservational interventions in India. A separate Department of Environment was established in 1980, and in 1985, it was upgraded to a full-fledged Ministry of Environment and Forests. The Ministry of Environment and Forests (MoEF) of the Government of India is the chief organization in India for ecological forecasting, advancement, regulation, and execution. Additional foremost assistances that support the MoEF in implementation ecofriendly-associated maneuvers contain:

- Union Territories (UT) Environmental Committees
- Central Pollution Control Board
- State Pollution Control Boards
- State Departments of Environment
- Central Pollution Control Board
- The Indian Forest Survey
- The Indian Wildlife Institute
- The Botanical and Zoological Survey of India
- The National Afforestation and Eco-development Board

CONSTITUTIONAL PROVISION OF ENVIRONMENTAL LAW

There are certain constitutional provisions which give certain power and rights to the citizens to protect environment.

Article 48A: This Article comes under the Directive principle of the State policy. This article implies that the government should make every effort to protect the environment. It also highlights the protection of the country's forests and animals. Article 48A imposes a duty on State to protect the environment from pollution by adopting various measures.

Article 51A (g): The Article 51 A(g) states that it shall be the duty of each and every Indian resident is responsible for preserving and improving the natural environment, which includes lakes, rivers, forests, and animals. This Article also focuses on showing compassion for living creatures. This article is similar to Article 48A, but the only difference is that it concentrates on fundamental duty of citizens whereas Article 48A instructs the state to perform their duties and protect environment. Hence, it is our duty to not only protect the environment from pollution but also improve its quality.

Article 253: This Article gives power to Parliament to create laws for the country in order to implement any treaty conventions and agreement with other countries. By this article, Parliament enacted various laws in order to protect environment like - Water Act 1974, Air Act 1981 and the Environmental Protection Act 1984.

Article 246: The Article 246 divides the subjects of legislation between Union and State. It also provides the details of Concurrent list in which both the Union and State make laws by sharing the jurisdiction comprising the protection of mines, wildlife and minerals development. So, both State and Union have power to enact laws to protect the environment. Article 246 also provides the extra power to Parliament in order to make laws in State list for the National interest.

Article 47: This article imposes duty on the State in order to improve the standards of living of citizens by providing health facilities, proper nutrition, and sanitization and protect the environment to live safely. Article 47 also pressurizes its citizens to be more conscious of the environment.

Article 21: It states that right to life is not just for animals but it also provides the right to humans to live safely in an environment with basic human dignities. Because Supreme Court had stated that the right to live includes living in a pollution-free environment and be free from diseases.

Article 19(1) (g): It states that citizens cannot practice such trade or business activities which are hazardous to public health.

Article 32 & 226: This article provides right to citizen to approach to Supreme or High Court whenever there is violation of fundamental right by PIL (Public Interest Litigation). This article helps preserve the environment and maintain ecological balance. This Article also dictates that environment conservation is not just the duty of government but also the responsibility of citizens of India.

MAJOR ENVIRONMENTAL ACTS AND RULES

Environmental law as a distinct system arose in the 1960s in the major industrial economies. It is fast becoming an important and specialized branch of law. The questions addressed to byenvironmental law are substantive in nature, whereas, the remedies of these issuesare mainly procedural. In recent years, environmental law has become seen as acritical means of promoting sustainable development. Policy concepts such as theprecautionary principle, public participation, environmental justice, and thepolluter pays principle have informed many environmental law reforms in thisrespect. There has been considerable experimentation in the search for moreeffective methods of environmental control beyond traditional "command-andcontrol" style regulation. Eco-taxes, tradable emission allowances, voluntarystandards such as ISO 14000 and negotiated agreements are some of theseinnovations. Some of the important environmental acts are a follow:

A. THE WATER (POLLUTION PREVENTION AND CONTROL) ACT OF 1974
B. THE AIR (POLLUTION PREVENTION AND CONTROL) ACT OF 1981
C. RULES FOR NOISE POLLUTION (REGULATION AND CONTROL) (AMENDMENT), 2010
D. ENVIRONMENTAL PROTECTION ACT OF 1986
E. THE 1972 WILDLIFE PROTECTION ACT
F. THE 1980 FOREST CONSERVATION ACT
G. THE BIOLOGICAL DIVERSITY ACT 2002 AND BIOLOGICAL DIVERSITY RULES
H. THE HAZARDOUS WASTES (MANAGEMENT AND HANDLING) RULES, 1989 & 2000.
A. PUBLIC LIABILITY INSURANCE ACT, 1991.
J. THE NATIONAL ENVIRONMENT TRIBUNAL ACT, 1995.
K. THE CHEMICAL ACCIDENTS (EMERGENCY PLANNING, PREPAREDNESS

AND RESPONSE RULES, 1996.

AX. THE BIOMEDICAL WASTES (MANAGEMENT AND HANDLING) RULES, 1998.

ALL. MUNICIPAL WASTES (PROCESS AND DISPOSAL) DRAFT RULES, 1999.
N. THE RECYCLED PLASTIC MANUFACTURE AND USAGE RULES, 1999.
O. THE FLY ASH NOTIFICATION, 1999.
P. THE BATTERIES (MANAGEMENT AND HANDLING (DRAFT) RULES, 2000.
Q. ENVIRONMENT (PROTECTION) AMENDMENT RULES, 2021

A. THE WATER (POLLUTION PREVENTION AND CONTROL) ACT OF 1974

The purpose of this legislation is to prevent and regulate water contamination, as well as to maintain or restore the wholesomeness of water. As a result, this Act covers all human activities that have an impact on water quality. Starved of the erstwhile consensus of the State Pollution Control Board (SPCB), no individual can begin any production, process, or handling and clearance scheme, or a leeway or adding thereto, that is probable to expulsion manure or profession waste into a torrent, healthy cesspit, or on pointer, and must smear to the SPCB fretful to gain the "assent to inaugurate" along with the "consensus to work" the diligence later launch.

THE WATER (POLLUTION PREVENTION AND CONTROL) CESS ACT OF 1977

The principal objective of this Act is to tariff and accumulate a cess on water utilised by particular industries as listed in the Act's schedule. CPCBs and SPCBs use the funds raised to prevent and control water pollution.

VIOLATIONS AND PENALTIES

Whoever contravenes any provision of this Act or fails to comply with any order or direction issued under this Act for which no penalty is provided elsewhere in this Act shall be punished by imprisonment for a period of three months or a fine of ten thousand rupees, or both, and in the case of a continuing contravention or failure, by an additional fine of five thousand rupees for each day during which the contravention or failure continues.

B. THE AIR (POLLUTION PREVENTION AND CONTROL) ACT OF 1981

The Air Act of 1981 was enacted with the goal of preventing, controlling, and reducing air pollution, including noise pollution. Under the terms of this Act, no person shall develop or operate any industrial plant in an air pollution control area without the prior authorization of the SPCB. The stockholder must put on to the SPCB/Pollution Control Committee (PCB) for agreement. No one functioning an industrialized plant is allowed to release any air pollution in excess of the SPCB's guidelines, and they must adhere to the rules.The Air (Prevention and Control of Pollution) Act, 1981 is a law passed by the Parliament of India in order to prevent and control the harmful effects of air pollution in India. This Act was passed by the government in 1981 in order to clean up the air by regulating pollution levels. According to the Air (Prevention and Control of Pollution) Act, 1981, power plants, vehicles and industries are not allowed to release particular matter, lead, carbon monoxide or other toxic substances beyond a prescribed level.

VIOLATIONS AND PENALTIES

Under Section 39, any order or direction which has been flouted, and for which there is no punishment anywhere in the Act, shall be punishable with three months' imprisonment or fine of three thousand rupees or both. If failure continues, there shall be a fine of an additional five thousand rupees every day.

RULES ON NOISE POLLUTION (REGULATION AND CONTROL) (AMENDMENT), 2010

These rules provide the criteria and conditions necessary to reduce noise pollution and to allow the use of loud speakers or public address systems at night or during any cultural or religious festival. At night, a loudspeaker, any sound producing device, or a sound amplifier may be used only in closed premises for internal communication, such as auditoriums, conference rooms, community halls, or banquet halls, or in the event of a public emergency. The noise level at the edge of the public space where a loudspeaker or public address system is being utilised should not exceed 10 decibels above the ambient noise requirements of that region, or 75 decibels, whichever is lower.Except in emergency cases, no horn shall be used in silent zones or residential neighborhoods at night. Construction equipment that emits noise is not permitted to work at night.

VIOLATIONS AND PENALTIES

According to the new fine rates, people can be fined up to Rupees 1 lakh for causing noise pollution. As per the new rule, the fine to be imposed on any individual burning firecrackers after the stipulated time is Rupees 1,000 in residential and commercial areas and Rupees 3,000 in silent zones.

D. ENVIRONMENTAL PROTECTION ACT OF 1986

This is a parasol Act for the fortification and development of the environment and its formatters, which states that no person conducting any industry, operation, or process shall discharge or emit, or permit to be discharged or emitted, any environmental pollutant in excess of such standards as may be prescribed. Several rules relating to the management of hazardous substances, wastes, and other materials have been published. The Central Government has rusticated, restricted the location of companies in several locations under this Act in order to keep the situation. Several ethics for air contaminants, sewage release, and sound have been established and issued.The Central Government has the buff to revenue any actions required to conserve and improve the environment, subject to the provisions of this Act. Procedures, protections, prohibitions and limitations on the supervision of perilous constituents, along with preventions and precincts on the locality of corporations in certain locations, have all been made public.

The Environment (Protection) Act, 1986 authorizes the central government to protect and improve environmental quality, control and reduce pollution from all sources, and prohibit or restrict the setting and /or operation of any industrial facility on environmental grounds. The Environment (Conservation) Act was passed in 1986 with the goal of ensuring environmental protection and enhancement. It gives the Central Government the authority to create authorities tasked with preventing all forms of environmental pollution and addressing specific environmental issues that are unique to different sections of the country. The last time the Act was changed was in 1991. The Environment (Protection) Rules lay down procedures for setting standards of emission or discharge of environmental pollutants. The Environment (Protection) Act of 1986 is one of the bare acts of environmental law that protects and improves the environment. The term 'environment' refers to elements such as air, water, and land, as well as the interactions between them, which include humans, microorganisms, and plants. The Environment Protection Act, 1986 had enacted this law at the United Nations Conference in order to protect the human environment.

VIOLATIONS AND PENALTIES

The Environmental Protection Act 1986 (EP Act), the umbrella Act for numerous rules adopted under it such as the waste rules, provides for only one type of punishment. Any breach of these rules is punishable with imprisonment for a term up to five years, or a fine up to Rupees 1 lakh, or both. Section 24 states that if an offence is punished under both the Environment Protection Act and another law, the person is not accountable under the Environment Protection Act.

E. THE 1972 WILDLIFE PROTECTION ACT

The Wild Life (Protection) Act of 1972 was enacted with the goal of efficiently conserving our country's wild life and controlling poaching, smuggling, and illicit wildlife and derivatives trade. The Act was revised in January 2003, making the penalties and punishments for violations of the Act more severe. The Ministry has suggested more changes to the law, including more stringent steps to reinforce it. The goal is to safeguard listed endangered flora and animals, as well as biologically significant protected areas.India's Wildlife Protection Act of 1972 is a comprehensive piece of legislation that regulates sanctuaries, national parks, and zoos among other protected locations.

VIOLATIONS AND PENALTIES

Illegal hunting in tiger reserves or any attempt to encroach on reserve lands in the country could soon incur a jail term of not less than seven years and a fine up to Rupees 50 lakhs further poachers having a second run in with the law could up for stiffer punishment as a deterrent. The law further specifies that certain offences will result in a sentence of not less than three years, but up to seven years in jail and also include a fine which shall not be less than Rupees 10,000.

F. THE FOREST CONSERVATION ACT OF 1980 (F.THE FOREST CONSERVATION ACT OF 1980)

The Forest Conservation Act of 1980 was passed in order to aid in the conservation of the country's forests.The Forest (Conservation) Act, 1980 was passed with the aim to protect the forests by controlling the rates of deforestation. The Forest (Conservation) Act, 1980 came into force on October 25, 1980. This Act was enacted to safeguard our country's forests. It prohibits the de-reservation of forests or the use of forest land for non-forest purposes without prior authorisation from the Central Government. To that end, the Act establishes the conditions for diverting forest land for non-forest activities. Forest rights are recognized under the Scheduled Tribes and Other Traditional Forest Dwellers (Recognition of Forest Rights) Act of 2006. The Indian Forest Act of 1927 codifies the law governing forests and the transportation of forest products and the duty leviable on timber and other forest-produce and it was introduced in India for the management and preservation of forest areas.

VIOLATIONS AND PENALTIES

The penalty for violating the Act's provisions is that anybody who violates or aids in the violation of any of the provisions of section 2 is subject to a period of imprisonment of up to fifteen days. If any person cuts down a tree due to any reason, without taking permission from the forest department, in that case, the accused shall be punished with a fine of Rupees. 10,000- or three-months imprisonment.

G. THE BIOLOGICAL DIVERSITY ACT OF 2002 AND THE BIOLOGICAL DIVERSITY RULES

India's attempt to implement the objectives expressed in the United Nations Convention on Biological Diversity (CBD), 1992, which affirms states' sovereign rights to use their own biological resources, resulted in the Biological Diversity Act of 2002. The Act strives to protect biological resources and associated knowledge while also making them more accessible in a sustainable manner. The National Biodiversity Authority, headquartered in Chennai, was established to carry out the Act's objectives.

The Biological Variety Act of 2002 and the Biological Diversity Rules ensure that biological diversity is conserved, that its components are used sustainably, and that the advantages of using biological resources and knowledge linked with it are shared fairly and equally. The following are some of the important clauses aimed at achieving the above: Prohibition on the export of Indian genetic material without prior clearance from the Indian government; Without the authorization of the Indian government, anyone claiming an Intellectual Property Right (IPR), such as a patent, over biodiversity or related information is prohibited. Regulations governing the gathering and use of biodiversity by Indian nationals, with local groups exempted; Measures for sharing the benefits of biodiversity utilisation, such as technological transfer, monetary rewards, shared research and development, joint IPR ownership, and so on; Measures to conserve and sustainably use biological resources, such as habitat and species preservation, project Environmental Impact Assessments (EIAs), and the integration of biodiversity into many departments' plans, programmes, and policies. Use of genetically modified organisms is regulated; Establishment of National, State, and Local Biodiversity Funds to assist conservation and benefit sharing; Biodiversity Management Committees (BMC) at the local village level, State Biodiversity Boards (SBB) at the state level, and a National Biodiversity Authority at the national level are all being established (NBA).

VIOLATIONS AND PENALTIES

If any person contravenes any direction given or order made by the Central Government, the State Government, the National Biodiversity Authority or the State Biodiversity Board for which no punishment has been separately provided under this Act, he/she shall be punished with a fine which may extend to one lakh rupees as per the BD Act, accessing Indian biological resources without the prior approval of the NBA, could render the officers in charge of a company, as well as the company, liable for punishment by way of imprisonment of up to five years and / or a fine of up to Rupees ten Lakhs.

H. THE HAZARDOUS WASTES (MANAGEMENT AND HANDLING) RULES, 1989 & 2000.

Hazardous Waste (Management and Management) Rules, 1989 aim to regulate hazardous waste generation, collection, treatment, import, storage, and handling. The Hazardous Chemicals Manufacture, Storage, and Import

Rules specify the terminologies used in this context and establishes an authority to inspect the industrial activity associated with hazardous chemicals and separated storage facilities once a year. The Manufacture, Use, Import, Export, and Storage of Hazardous Microorganisms/ Genetically Engineered Organisms or Cells Rules, 1989 were enacted to protect the environment, nature, and human health when gene technology and microorganisms were applied. Hazardous wastes are divided into 18 categories. According to this decree, scheme protagonists handling precarious waste must tale to the suitable establishments, obtain authorization to handle wastes, keep proper records, file annual returns, label all packages, consignments, and other items, and report any accident immediately in order to report hazardous waste import-export. On January 6, 2000, the Ministry of Environment and Forestry (MOEF) issued the HW (M&H) Adjustment Rules (MoEF, 2000a). Noxious compounds, burnable compounds, and explosives have all been redefined as 'hazardous chemicals' under this law. There are 684 dangerous compounds present, according to the revised criterion.

Under these standards, project proponents in any hazardous business must evaluate potential hazards and take appropriate measures to avoid and allay the concerns of any on-site fortune. Material Safety Data Sheets (MSDS) must be generated for all substances handled. Workers must be supplied with knowledge, training, and the essential equipment to ensure their safety on the job. Before beginning any operation at the site, an onsite emergency plan should be created. For any mishap that may occur on site, the District Controller will establish an off-site emergency plan in nigh discussion with the plan exponents. The civic in the zone of the ability should be learned around the environment of any major accidents that may occur on site, as well as the Do's and Don'ts that should be followed in the event of one. Hazardous chemical imports must be notified to the appropriate authority within 30 days of the date of import. On January 20, 2000, the Ministry of Environment and Forestry (MOEF) announced substantial changes to the Manufacture, Storage, and Import of Hazardous Chemical Rules (MSIHC Rules), 1989. Renewal of authorization will be contingent on the filing of 'Annual Returns' for hazardous waste disposal, a reduction in waste created, recycled, or reused, compliance with authorization criteria, and payment of a remittance processing and analysis fee. The designation location for a common waste disposal facility shall be the responsibility of the state government as well as the occupant or its association. Before informing any common hazardous waste disposal site, the state government is required to hold a public hearing. Design, operation, and closing of a shared waste facility/landfill site will be guided by the federal/state governments. Prior permission from the SPCB is required for the design and layout of the planned hazardous waste disposal plant.

VIOLATIONS AND PENALTIES

The occupier or operator of a facility shall ensure that the hazardous wastes are packaged, based on the composition in a manner suitable for handling, storage and transport and the labelling and packaging shall be easily visible and be able to withstand physical conditions and climatic factors.

The Central Pollution Control Board may cancel or suspend a registration or renewal granted under these rules, if in its opinion the registered recycler has failed to comply with any of the registration conditions or any of the Act's provisions or rules made thereunder after giving him an opportunity of being heard and after recording the reasons. Section 9 (3) of the Act embodies the "Polluter Pays Principle" which states that any expense which has been incurred to restore the environment to its natural state shall be paid by the person who is responsible for such degradation. This concept of a continuing punishment is very important.

I. PUBLIC LIABILITY INSURANCE ACT, 1991.

The fundamental goal of the Public Liability Insurance Act of 1991 is to compensate victims of accidents resulting from the handling of any dangerous chemical. All proprietors involved in the manufacture or handling of hazardous chemicals are subject to the Act. This Act, which is unique to India, makes the owner liable for immediate relief in the event of death or property damage caused by an accident when handling any of the specified hazardous chemicals. This assistance must be supplied on a "no fault" basis. The owner of a hazardous chemical must have insurance coverage in a quantity equivalent to its "waged up money" or up to Rs. 500 million, whichever is greater, to cover this risk. Every year, the policy must be renewed. Before beginning their business, new ventures must adopt this policy. The owner must also pay a sum equal to the annual premium to the Environment Chief Fund of the Central Government (ERF). Medical expenditures up to Rs. 12,500/- would be reimbursed. The insurance's responsibility is based on Rupees: 50 million per accident up to Rupees.

150 million every year or for the duration of the contract. The Emissions Reduction Fund will cover any claims related to this liability (ERF). If the award is still insufficient, the owner will be responsible for the balance. The cash made under the Act is only for immediate relief; owners are responsible for any compensation resulting from legal proceedings.

VIOLATIONS AND PENALTIES

According to the Public Liability Insurance Act, company owners must take out an insurance policy with hazardous substances within one year after starting work. He/she will be punished by imprisonment for up to three months, a fine of up to ten thousand rupees, or both.

J. THE NATIONAL ENVIRONMENT TRIBUNAL ACT, 1995.

The National Environmental Tribunal Act, as amended in 2010, was enacted in 1995. The Act was enacted to provide compensation for losses to people, property, and the environment caused by hazardous material activities. The Green Tribunal Act's three main goals are: I the effective and timely resolution of matters involving environmental protection and forest and other natural resource conservation. The Tribunal will also hear all of the previous pending cases.

ii) Its goal is to ensure that all environmental legal rights are upheld.

iii) It also accounts for offering compensation and aid to those who have suffered property damage.

The following are the key characteristics of amendment:

Any Indian citizen has the right to file a complaint with the National Green Tribunal under the amendment. It assures that when hearing appeals and issuing judgements, the tribunal considers concepts of Sustainable Development, Precautionary Principles, Polluter Pays Principles, and Intergenerational Equity.

Under the National Green Tribunal Act of 2010, the National Green Tribunal is responsible for the effective and timely resolution of cases involving environmental protection, forest conservation, and other natural resource conservation, as well as the enforcement of any legal right relating to the environment and the provision of relief and compensation for damages to persons and property, as well as matters related to or incidental to these matters. It is a specialist organization with the knowledge and experience to resolve environmental disputes involving many disciplines. The Tribunal will not be constrained by the method outlined in the Code of Civil Procedure, 1908, but will instead be guided by natural justice principles. The Tribunal's dedicated environmental jurisdiction will expedite environmental justice while also reducing the burden of litigation in the higher courts. The Tribunal is required to make and make every effort to resolve petitions or appeals within six months of their submission. Initially, the NGT will be set up in five locations and will operate on a circuit system to make itself more accessible. The Tribunal's Principal Place of Sitting is New Delhi, and the other four places of sitting are Bhopal, Pune, Kolkata, and Chennai. The National Environment Tribunal Act of 1995 was enacted to provide for strict liability for damages resulting from incidents occurring during the handling of hazardous substances, as well as the establishment of a National Environment Tribunal to handle cases arising from such incidents, with the goal of providing relief and compensation to people and the environment. The National Green Tribunal Act of 2010 ensures the effective and timely resolution of matters involving forest conservation, environmental preservation, and the enforcement of any environmental legal claim. In addition, the Act provides adequate compensation and remedies for losses to individuals and property, as well as related problems. The Act specifies the tribunal's jurisdiction, powers, and processes, as well as the consequences for violations.

VIOLATIONS AND PENALTIES

Failure to comply with Tribunal rulings carries a penalty of three years in prison, a fine of 10 lakh rupees, or both.

K. THE CHEMICAL ACCIDENTS (EMERGENCY PLANNING, PREPAREDNESS

AND RESPONSE RULES, 1996.

These rules established a legislative backup for the formation of a Crisis Group in districts and states with Major Accident Hazard (MAH) installations for the purpose of delivering public information. The MAH installations are defined by the rules, which comprise industrial activity, transportation, and segregated storage at a site handling hazardous chemicals in regulated quantities. The Government of India has established a Central Crisis Group (CCG) for the handling of chemical mishaps and has put up an alert system in accordance with the guidelines. Standing State Crisis Groups (SSCG) have also been established by the Chief Secretaries of all states to idea and retort to chemical events in the state. Districts must be prearranged as Local Central Crisis Groups by the District Controller (DCG and LCG). The CCG is the country's highest body for dealing with and providing professional advice chaired by the Chief Secretary. for major chemical accidents planning and handling. It continuously monitors post-accident saturation and provides preventative steps to avoid such mishaps.

The Ministry of External Affairs, Government of India, has issued a list of experts and concerned officials per state. The state's supreme body is presided by the Chief Secretary. The group, which is prepared up of GOI bureaucrats, practical specialists, and production legislatures, ponders on chemical accident scheduling, willingness, and vindication in order to diminish the damage of lifetime, possessions, and fitness. The SSCG evaluates the district's off-site substitute shrubberies for their appropriateness. The Chairman of the DCG, which serves as the apex body at the district level, is the District Collector. Every year, DCG will evaluate all on-Emergency shrubberies established by the MAH fittings' tenants and mien one complete of the off-cist Extra idea at a site. These guidelines allow for the creation of on-site and off-site emergency plans, as well as the upgrading and conduct of mock drills.

VIOLATIONS AND PENALTIES

Chemical safety includes all those policies, procedures and practices designed to minimize the risk of exposure to potentially hazardous chemicals. This includes the risks of exposure to persons handling the chemicals, to the surrounding environment, and to the communities and ecosystems within that environment. The State Crisis Group shall be the apex body in the State to deal with major chemical accidents and to provide expert guidance for handling major chemical accidents.

K. THE BIOMEDICAL WASTES (MANAGEMENT AND HANDLING) RULES, 1998.

The Biomedical Waste (Management and Handling) Rules, 1998 govern the disposal of biomedical wastes, such as anatomical waste, blood, body fluids, medicines, glass wares, and animal wastes, by health-care institutions in conurbations with populations of more than 30 lakh people or hospitals with more than 500 beds. They must install and commission necessary facilities for the treatment of biomedical waste, such as incinerators, autoclaves, and microwave systems. All people who deal with such issues must first get permission from the proper authority. Biomedical waste has been segregated at the source for all institutions and organizations that deal with it. These rules hold biomedical waste generators accountable for properly segregating, packing, storing, transporting, treating, and disposing of biomedical waste.

VIOLATIONS AND PENALTIES

According to the biomedical Waste (Management and Handling) Rules 1998, it is obligatory for hospitals, clinics, and different medical and veterinary institutes to eliminate biomedical wastes strictly in accordance with the guidelines of the government. Failure to dispose of medical waste as per the new rules will attract a jail term of five years or a fine of Rupees 1 lakh or both.

AX. MUNICIPAL WASTES (PROCESS AND DISPOSAL) DRAFT RULES, 1999.

The municipal authority is responsible for enforcing the terms of these rules, as well as any structural development for the gathering, stowing, ghettoization, transference, treating, and removal of MSW, and for warranting acquiescence with these rubrics. Municipal authorities must submit an annual report to the District Magistrate/Deputy Commissioner, who will have the ability to enforce these restrictions. MSW must be disposed of in a landfill according to established requirements and norms. Municipal authorities must adhere to the composting and treated leachate disposal criteria.

VIOLATIONS AND PENALTIES

An inefficient municipal solid waste management system may create serious negative environmental impacts like infectious diseases, land and water pollution, obstruction of drains and loss of biodiversity. No non-recyclable waste having a calorific value of 1,500 Kcal/kg or more is permitted in landfills. These wastes should either be utilized for generating energy or for preparing refuse derived fuel. It may also be used for co-processing in cement or thermal power plants. Urban local bodies have been given a provision to charge bulk generators a user fee to collect and process their waste. Additionally spot fines may be levied on people burning garbage or discarding it in public places.

N. THE RECYCLED PLASTIC MANUFACTURE AND USAGE RULES, 1999.

The use of carry bags or containers made of recycled plastics for storing, carrying, dispensing, or packing food is prohibited under these regulations. Plastic carry bags or containers can only be made if I virgin plastic is used in its normal dimness or white, and (ii) reprocessed pliable is recycled for usages other than stowing and padding fodder with tinctures and colorants, as per IS: 9833:1981. The Bureau of Indian Standards Specification IS: 14534: 1998, titled "The Guideline for Recycling of Plastics," must be rigorously followed while recycling plastics. 'Made of Recycled Material' or'Virgin Plastic' must be printed on each package of carry bags by the manufacturer. A carry bag's minimum thickness should not be less than 20 microns. Finally, the Plastic Industry Association must implement self-regulatory steps through its member units.

VIOLATIONS AND PENALTIES

Recycling of plastic waste must conform to the Indian Standard: IS 14534:1998 titled as Guidelines for Recycling of Plastics, as amended from time to time; The provision of thickness must not be applicable to carry bags made up of compostable plastic. State Pollution Control Board or the Pollution Control Committees shall not revoke, suspend or cancel registration without providing the opportunity of a hearing to the produceror person engaged in recycling or processing of plastic wastes. Every retailer or street vendors selling or providing commodities in, plastic carry bags or multilayered packaging or plastic sheets or like or covers made of plastic sheets which are not manufactured or labelled or marked in accordance with these rules shall be liable to pay such fines as specified under the laws of the local bodies.

O. THE FLY ASH NOTIFICATION, 1999.

Fly ash is the residue of coal combustion, which, if disposed of improperly, is hazardous for health and the environment due to the concentrated presence of heavy metals. The Fly Ash notification (1999) mandates the use of fly ash for the purpose of manufacturing ash-based products such as cement, concrete blocks, bricks, panels or any other material or for construction of roads, embankments, dams or for any other construction activity within a radius of 300 km from thermal power stations (TPPs). Besides, it is also mandatory to use fly ash in the external overburden, mines backfilling or stowing of mines within a distance of 50 km. It is also mandatory for all construction agencies/Government Departments undertaking road projects, fly over/ bridges as well as local authorities to make provisions for use of fly ash in their tender documents and schedule of material and rates. The notification also prescribes the targets for Fly Ash utilization in a phased manner for all Coal/Lignite based TPPs in the country so as to achieve 100% utilization of fly ash.

On September 14, 1999, a notice was issued to preserve mud and limit the abandoning and removal of fly ash emanated from coal or lignite-built thermal power facilities. In order to manufacture clay bricks, tiles, or blocks used in building activities, every brick manufacturer within a 50-kilometer radius of a coal or lignite-based thermal power plant must mix at least 25% ash (fly ash/bottom ash/pond ash) with soil on a weight-to-weight ratio. Every coal or lignite-based thermal power station must make ash available for producing ash-based products for as a minimum ten years from the date of publication of this announcement, without compensation or other assistance. Every coal or lignite-based thermal power station that is bespoke underneath ecological settings that involve the suggestion of a deed idea must ensure so within nine years (15 years for plants not covered by environmental clearance). According to the regulation, central and state government agencies, state electricity boards, NTPC, and thermal power plant management must include ash and ash-based products in their schedules of requirements. All local governments must also stipulate the use of ash and ash-based goods in their individual building bylaws and regulations.

VIOLATIONS AND PENALTIES

Under new rules, notified by the environment ministry, non-compliant power plants will be imposed with an environmental compensation of Rupees 1,000 per tonne on unutilized ash during the end of every financial year. The Union Ministry of Environment, Forest and Climate Change (MoEF&CC) issued a draft notification on December 3, 2020 for utilization of fly ash by coal- and lignite-based power plants. Apart from the penalty structure, the draft also mandates that all power plants sharethe real-time data on ash availability with CPCB. Measures for ash utilization by new thermal plants and all mines have also been outlined in the draft, along with ash pond maintenance guidelines. The draft specifies a fine of Rupees 1,000 per tonne of unutilized ash if the plant does not achieve at least 80 per cent ash utilization annually or in three years. An additional fine of Rupees 1,000 per tonne will also be imposed for failing to adhere to progressive utilization at least 20 per cent in first year, 35 per cent in the second, 50 per cent in the third to tenth.

P. THE BATTERIES (MANAGEMENT AND HANDLING (DRAFT) RULES, 2000.

To combat the dangers of backyard smelting and unlawful reprocessing of lead acid batteries, the MoEF developed the Batteries (M&H) (Draft)

Rules, 2000. Automobiles such as cars, trucks, buses, two wheelers, and inverters all require lead acid batteries. Battery manufacturers, importers, assemblers, and reconditioners must collect old batteries on a one-to-one basis against the sale of new batteries, according to the requirement. Unless the battery manufacturers have such recycling facilities, the batteries must be sent to recyclers who have registered with the MoEF to recycle them in an environmentally acceptable manner. Only those units that have acceptable production technologies, pollution protection methods, and waste disposal procedures are allowed to register with the MoEF. Importers of new batteries, dealers, and organizations that auction used batteries have all been subjected to these laws. Only re-processors who have registered with the MoEF will be permitted to participate in the auction or contract sale. As a result, intermediaries and backyard smelters are no longer permitted to participate in any auctions in the United States. Manufacturers must provide appropriate options for buyback in the event that they sell batteries in bulk to large groups of people. Recycling ferrous metals like lead and zinc saves energy in principal metal manufacture and is ecologically positive if reclaiming is completed with applicable contamination regulator and leftover removal systems, as well as helping to conserve precious metal resources.

VIOLATIONS AND PENALTIES

Button batteries should be disposed at hazardous waste collection sites. Similarly, rechargeable Lead-Acid or Nickel Cadmium batteries should also be disposed at household hazardous waste collection sites. Lithium or Lithium-Ion batteries can be dropped off at nearby battery recycling centers. Whoever fails to comply with or contravenes any of the provisions of this Act, or the rules made, orders or directions issued thereunder, shall be punished, in respect of each such failure or contravention, with imprisonment for a term up to 5 years, a fine up to Rs.100000/-, or both, and, if the failure or contravention continues, with an additional fine up to Rs.5000/- for each day during which such failure or contravention continues. If the failure or violation continues for more than one year from the date of conviction, the offender will be sentenced to prison for a term of up to seven years.

R. THE OZONE DEPLETING SUBSTANCES (REGULATION AND CONTROL) RULES, 2000

The Ozone Depleting substances (Regulation and Control) Rules, 2000, and its amendments, have been published by the Central Government in the Gazette of India, under Environment (Protection) Act, 1986. India introduced the licensing system in 1996, based on recommendation of the Meeting of Parties at Geneva in 1995. Our country is now focusing attention on phasing out such chemicals in foam, refrigeration and halon sector. The main effect of ozone depletion is an increase in UV-B rays reaching the earth's surface. Chlorofluorocarbon (CFCs), halons, and other compounds deplete the ozone layer. CFCs and halons break down into chlorine and bromine which in turn destroy the ozone layer.Production and import of these chemicals is controlled by the Montreal Protocol on Substances that Deplete the Ozone Layer (the Montreal Protocol). There are other ozone depleting substances, but their ozone depleting effects are very small, so they are not controlled by the Montreal Protocol. The rules consist of 14 basic rules and 12 schedules which mentiondifferent provisions related to the phase out dates, consumption, importation, export of Ozone Depleting Substances, licensing of agencies, use of thesesubstances in different products, and other provisions. The various products that are made out of Ozone Depleting Substancesare Automobile and truck air-conditioning units (whether incorporated in vehicle ornot), Domestic and commercial refrigeration and air-conditioning/heat pumpequipment like refrigerators, dehumidifiers, freezers, water coolers, icemachines, air conditioning and heat pump units, compressors. Aerosol products (except medical aerosols) Portable fire extinguishers, Insulation boards, panels, pipe covers andPre-polymers.

VIOLATIONS AND PENALTIES

United Nations Development Programme (UNDP) is supporting the Government of India in phasing out (HCFCs) **by 2030**, as part of the country's commitment to the Montreal Protocol. The Montreal Protocol sets binding progressive phase out obligations for developed and developing countries for all the major ozone depleting substances, including chlorofluorocarbons (CFCs), halons and less damaging transitional chemicals such as hydro chlorofluorocarbons (HCFCs).

Q.ENVIRONMENT (PROTECTION) AMENDMENT RULES, 2021

The Ministry of Environment, Forest and Climate Change on June 16, 2021, has issued the Environment (Protection) Amendment Rules, 2021 to further amend the Environment (Protection) Rules, 1986. The following amendment has been made: Rule 5(3)(d), which specifies the time duration for Central Government to consider objections and impose restrictions/ prohibitions. "Provided that on account of COVID-19 pandemic, for the purpose of this clause, the period of validity of the notification expiring in the financial year 2020-2021 and 2021-2022 shall be extended up to December 31, 2021 or six months from the end of the month when the relevant notification would have expired without any extension, whichever is later."

VIOLATIONS AND PENALTIES

The act promulgates the liability for causing pollution, whether the pollution is caused by individual or by a corporation, such causing may be civil or criminal. Whoever fails to comply with or contravenes any of the provisions of this Act, or the rules adopted, orders or directions issued thereunder, shall be punished by imprisonment for a term of up to five years or a fine of up to one lakh for each such failure or violation No Court shall take notice of any infraction under this Act unless the Central Government or any authority acting on its behalf files a complaint. A individual who has petitioned the courts after the Central Government or an authority acting on its behalf has been served with a 60-day notice.

ENVIRONMENTAL PROTECTION AND INDIAN PENAL CODE

There are various sections in the Indian Penal Code, 1860 that make polluting the environment punishable. They can be used to prevent pollution in the environment. Chapter XIV of the IPC, containing Section 268-294-A, deals with the offences that are related to safety, public health, etc. These provisions make public health a priority and make any act punishable which pollutes the environment and makes the life of an individual dangerous. Section 268 defines the term public nuisance and says that:If any person does any illegal act, or omission then he/she is guilty of an offence. Such an act must have caused a 'common injury' or danger. Annoyance to the public, or to the people of a vicinity, or such an act must violate someone's public right. A common nuisance is not excused on the ground that it causes some convenience or advantage. Section 278 of the IPC states that anyone who voluntarily vitiate or spoil the atmosphere of any place in order to make it noxious for the health of persons living or doing business or passing along a public way, should be punished with a fine up to Rupees. 500. Moreover, Section 290 makes the offence of public nuisance punishable with a fine extending up to Rupees. 200. Therefore, if any act or omission of polluting the environment is committed harming any citizen then the same shall be subject to prosecution. Section 290 also makes noise pollution an offence. Section 277 of IPC states that if anyone who voluntarily corrupts or fouls the water of public spring or reservoir, so as to make it unfit for ordinary public use, shall be held punishable with imprisonment for up to 3 months or with fine up to Rupees. 1000 or with both. According to Section 278, whoever voluntarily vitiates (spoils) the atmosphere of any place so as to make it harmful for any person's health in a general dwelling, or carrying on a business in a neighborhood or passing along the public way, shall be liable to a fine of up to Rupees. 500.

After the Stockholm Conference, the declaration on the human environment was adopted. It was the first step towards conservation and protection of the environment at an international level. As per the declaration, states were required to make legislations and take legislative measures to protect and improve the environment. After the declaration, Article 48A was added as the Directive Principle of State Policy along with Article 51A through the Constitution (42nd Amendment) Act, 1976 making the duty of government and the citizens to protect the environment.

PUBLIC AWARENESS ON ENVIRONMENT

As we know public awareness is the most effective and fruitful to protect our environment andit's always better than laws, rules and regulations. Because of without awareness and support ofhuman beings, any law can't give good result. The environment sensitivity in our country canonly grow through a public awareness programmes. This has several tools like the electronicmedia, the press, schools & college education, adult education which are all essentiallycomplimentary to each other green movements can grow out of small local initiatives to welcomemajor players in advocating environmental protection to the government.

Environmental awareness is to understand the fragility of environment and the importance of its protection. Promoting environmental awareness is an easy way to become an environmental steward and participate in creating a brighter future for coming generations. Environmental campaign has become an important tool to achieve effective compliance of various pollution control norms. Large scale public involvement can strengthen environment movements for the sake of implementation of environment-friendly rules and regulations by the government machinery in much better way to have the most desired results.

ENVIRONMENTAL LEGISLATION

1972 June 5th Environment was first discussed as an agenda in UN conference on Human Environment. There after every year 5th June is celebrated as Environment Day.

CONSTITUTIONAL PROVISIONS

Added in 1976 Article 48A "The state shall endeavor to protect and improve the environment and to safeguard forests and wildlife of the country"

Article 51A (g): "It shall be the duty of every citizen of India to protect and improve the natural environment including forests, lakes, rivers and wildlife and to have compassion for living creatures". By these two articles one constitution makes environment protection and conservation as one of our fundamental duties.

CENTRAL POLLUTION CONTROL BOARD (CPCB)

1.Advices CG in matters, prevention and control of water pollution.

2.Coordinates SPCB and provide technical assistance and guidance.

3.Training programs for prevention and control of pollution by mass media and other ways.

4.Publishes statistical and technical details about pollution.

5.Prepares manual for treatment and disposal of sewerage and trade effluents.

6.Lays standard for water quality parameters.

7.Plans nation-wide programs for prevention, control or abatement of pollution.

8.Laboratories for analysis of water, sewage or trade effluents.

STATE POLLUTION CONTROL BOARD (SPCB)

SPCB has similar functions as SPCB and governed by CPCB

1.SPCB advises state government with respect to location of any industry that might pollute.

2.Lays standard for effluents to take samples from streams, wells or trade effluents or sewage passing through an industry. Samples taken are analyzed at recognized labs. If the sample is not confirming to the water quality standard, then the unit is neglected.

3. Every industry to obtain consent from PCB before commencing an effluent unit by applying in prescribed form with fee.

ENFORCEMENT OF ENVIRONMENTAL LEGISLATION MAJOR ISSUES

1. Target of 33% of land to be covered by forest not achieved.
2. Rivers turning to open sewers.
3. Big towns and cities polluted.
4. Wild life endangered.

5. EFP (Effluent Treatment Plant) or Air Pollution Control devices are expensive leads to closure of units. Government should provide subsidy for small units.

6. Pollution control laws not backed up by policy pronouncements or guidelines

7. Chairman of PCB political nominee. Hence political interference.

8. Involving public in decision making envisaged by policy statement of the ministry of environment and forest (1992) is only in paper.

Because it is the vital liability of residents to defend and protect the surroundings, as cherished in our Establishment, legislation only is not the resolution to conservational organization. It is the accountability of all people to attempt to defend the situation for existing and imminent cohorts. Because environmental degradation affects us all, environmental regulation is basically a social law. Pollution offences must be taken severely because they are criminal. The framework for disciplinary action against violators is provided by environmental legislation. Safeguarding, salvaging, and reprocess are present drifts in the mechanism of some Actions of Indian legislature, and a comprehensive resource conservation and recovery act is urgently needed today. It is not necessarily essential for environmental deterioration or hazard to arise in order for the law to be implemented. Before such events, one should constantly take precautions. Environmental degradation is a difficult issue that necessitates a multifaceted approach. There are few environmental protection regulations, but we need a strong hand to put them in place. Environmental education can help to mitigate the negative consequences of pollution.

Conclussion

The existence and strict implementation of environmental laws are crucial for the conservation and protection of the environment and wildlife. The Indian Constitution, through Articles 48-A and 51-A, mandates both the government and citizens to safeguard and improve the environment. The Ministry of Environment and Forests (MoEF), established post the Stockholm Conference of 1972, plays a pivotal role in regulating and preserving the natural environment. Despite significant progress, challenges remain in achieving comprehensive environmental protection. India's environmental legislation, including the Water Act of 1974, Air Act of 1981, and Environmental Protection Act of 1986, provides a robust framework for pollution control and conservation efforts. Additionally, the Wildlife Protection Act of 1972 and various other regulations underscore the importance of protecting biodiversity. Effective enforcement of these laws, coupled with public awareness and education, is essential for sustainable development. The collective responsibility of the government, citizens, and international commitments ensures that environmental conservation is prioritized, fostering a healthier and more sustainable future for all.

Summary

Sent by Copilot:

Summary

Environmental laws and their strict implementation are essential for the conservation and protection of the environment and wildlife. The Indian Constitution, through Article 48-A (Directive Principles of State Policy), mandates the government to maintain and improve the environment and wildlife. Article 51-A (Fundamental Duties) imposes a duty on citizens to preserve and improve the natural environment. India has also made several international commitments and signed treaties for environmental protection.

The Ministry of Environment and Forests (MoEF), established in 1985 after the Stockholm Conference of 1972, is a key body for environmental protection in India. It regulates and preserves the natural environment and legislates on the legal and regulatory framework. The MoEF, along with the Pollution Control Board, forms the administrative core of this sector. Despite significant progress, challenges remain in achieving comprehensive environmental protection.

The environmental sector has advanced globally and in India, but further improvements and reforms are needed. Environmental legislation is crucial as, without adequate regulations and laws, environmental conservation cannot be realized. Creating environmental awareness and promoting environmental education are vital to ensure humans conserve the environment for the future.

Major Environmental Policies and Legislations in India

The MoEF is the nodal body in the Central Government's administrative structure for planning, promotion, coordination, and oversight of environmental and forestry programs. It is also the nodal agency for the United Nations Environment Programme (UNEP). The Ministry's principal activities include conservation and survey of flora, fauna, forests, and wildlife, pollution prevention and control, afforestation, and regeneration of degraded areas. The main tools used include surveys, impact assessments, pollution control, regeneration programs, support to organizations, research, training, and environmental awareness creation.

Key Environmental Acts and Rules

The Water (Prevention and Control of Pollution) Act of 1974: Established the Central Pollution Control Board (CPCB) to promote cleanliness of streams and wells and control water pollution.

The Air (Prevention and Control of Pollution) Act of 1981: Aims to prevent, control, and reduce air pollution, including noise pollution.

Rules for Noise Pollution (Regulation and Control) (Amendment), 2010: Provides criteria and conditions to reduce noise pollution.

Environmental Protection Act of 1986: A comprehensive act for the protection and improvement of the environment.

The Wildlife Protection Act of 1972: Aims to conserve wildlife and control poaching, smuggling, and illegal trade of wildlife and derivatives.

Constitutional Provisions for Environmental Law

Article 48A: Directs the state to protect and improve the environment and safeguard forests and wildlife.

Article 51A(g): Imposes a duty on citizens to protect and improve the natural environment.

Article 253: Empowers Parliament to make laws for implementing international treaties and agreements.

Article 246: Divides legislative subjects between Union and State, allowing both to enact laws for environmental protection.

Article 47: Directs the state to improve public health and nutrition and protect the environment.

Article 21: Ensures the right to a pollution-free environment as part of the right to life.

Article 19(1)(g): Restricts hazardous trade or business activities.

Articles 32 & 226: Allow citizens to approach courts for the enforcement of fundamental rights, including environmental protection.

These laws and constitutional provisions highlight the importance of environmental protection and the collective responsibility of the government and citizens to ensure a sustainable future.

www.ingramcontent.com/pod-product-compliance
Lightning Source LLC
LaVergne TN
LVHW021202160826
845679LV00024B/2209

* 9 7 9 8 8 9 5 8 8 5 8 2 6 *